TEAM SPIRIT®

SMART BOOKS FOR YOUNG FANS

THE CHICAGO BULLS

BY
MARK STEWART

NORWOODHOUSE PRESS
CHICAGO, ILLINOIS

Norwood House Press
P.O. Box 316598
Chicago, Illinois 60631

For information regarding Norwood House Press, please visit our website at:
www.norwoodhousepress.com or call 866-565-2900.

All photos courtesy of Associated Press except the following:
Chicago Bulls (6, 33, 43 bottom), Topps, Inc. (7, 9, 15, 22, 23, 42 both, 43 top, 45),
Black Book Partners (17, 25, 34), The New York Times Company (18), Cincinnati Royals (21),
TIME Inc./Sports Illustrated (37, 38), NBA Players Association (39).
Cover Photo: Nam Y. Huh/Associated Press

The memorabilia and artifacts pictured in this book are presented for educational and informational purposes,
and come from the collection of the author.

Editor: Mike Kennedy
Designer: Ron Jaffe
Project Management: Black Book Partners, LLC.
Special thanks to Topps, Inc.

Library of Congress Cataloging-in-Publication Data

Stewart, Mark, 1960 July 7-
  The Chicago Bulls / by Mark Stewart. -- Revised edition.
    pages cm. -- (Team spirit)
  Includes bibliographical references and index.
  Summary: "A revised Team Spirit Basketball edition featuring the Chicago
Bulls that chronicles the history and accomplishments of the team. Includes
access to the Team Spirit website which provides additional information and
photos"-- Provided by publisher.
  ISBN 978-1-59953-631-6 (library edition : alk. paper) -- ISBN
978-1-60357-640-6 (ebook) 1. Chicago Bulls (Basketball
team)--History--Juvenile literature. I. Title.
  GV885.52.C45S74 2014
  796.323'640977311--dc23
                                            2014005654

253N—072014
Manufactured in the United States of America in North Mankato, Minnesota.

COVER PHOTO: The Bulls have established a tradition of winning, thanks to stars such as
Joakim Noah and Derrick Rose.

Table of Contents

ABOUT OUR GLOSSARY

In this book, there may be several words that you are reading for the first time. Some are sports words, some are new vocabulary words, and some are familiar words that are used in an unusual way. All of these words are defined on page 46. Throughout the book, sports words appear in **bold type**. Regular vocabulary words appear in ***bold italic type***.

Basketball fans love to look at statistics. Even so, numbers don't tell you everything about a team. The Chicago Bulls are proof of this. They won six championships during the 1990s. And though the Bulls of this *era* had the game's greatest player, the secret to their success was teamwork.

That type of team spirit has been a *tradition* in Chicago since the team's first season in the **National Basketball Association (NBA)**. The Bulls play with fire and intelligence. They work hard on defense and fight for every rebound. And they never give up.

This book tells the story of the Bulls. When a game comes down to a few crucial plays, they do all the little things that add up to victory. The Bulls are known for helping one another, making sacrifices, and blending their talents to win. Those are the things that statistics can never measure.

Taj Gibson hugs Tony Snell after a last-second victory during the 2013–14 season.

The city of Chicago, Illinois, has a love affair with basketball that stretches back more than a *century*. High school and college teams have always been popular in and around the "Windy City." **Professional** teams have called Chicago home since the 1920s. However, it was not until the Bulls came to town in 1966 that Chicago sports fans truly embraced a pro team.

The Bulls joined the NBA when it expanded from nine teams to ten. As a new club, Chicago had to find creative ways to build its roster. The Bulls looked to players that other NBA teams no longer valued. Among these cast-offs were a handful of stars, including guards Guy Rodgers and Jerry Sloan, and forward Bob Boozer.

The Bulls were also awarded the last pick in each round of the NBA **draft**. Despite its patchwork roster, Chicago was able to hold its own during its first season. The Bulls finished with more victories than any **expansion club** before or since.

During the 1970s, the Bulls continued to improve. Their best player was Bob Love, a forward who could score, rebound, and play tough defense. Love led the Bulls in points seven years in a row. Chicago also had one of the NBA's top one-on-one players in forward Chet Walker. Point guard Norm Van Lier led the club from the backcourt. Teammates and fans called him "Stormin' Norman," because of his intense desire to win. Chicago's defense was helped by centers Tom Boerwinkle, Clifford Ray, and Nate Thurmond. The Bulls made it to the finals of the **Eastern Conference** in 1973–74, and again the following season.

Later in the 1970s, the Bulls added more stars, including Artis Gilmore, Mickey Johnson, David Greenwood, and Reggie Theus. Two more impact players, Quintin Dailey and Orlando Woolridge, joined the team in the 1980s. Unfortunately, Chicago was unable

LEFT: Bob Boozer was an original member of the Bulls.
ABOVE: This trading card features some of Chicago's top players of the 1970s.

to repeat its earlier success. Things began to change in 1984, when the Bulls used the third pick in the NBA draft to select college star Michael Jordan.

There seemed to be no limit to Jordan's talent. He was named **Rookie of the Year** in 1984–85 and was the league's top scorer seven years in a row starting in his third season. Jordan was such an amazing player that his teammates often faded into the background. This prevented the Bulls from reaching

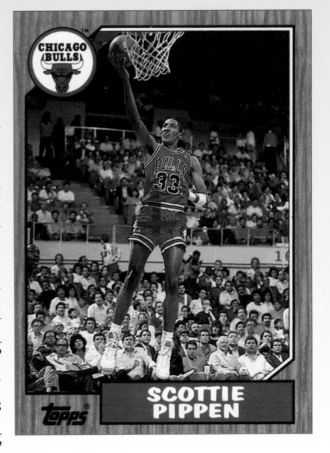

the **NBA Finals** during the 1980s. More balanced, team-oriented opponents always defeated them in the **playoffs**.

The Bulls finally became a great team during the 1990s, when they found the right players to surround Jordan. Scottie Pippen was a wonderful all-around forward who worked hard on offense and defense. He led a group of talented supporting players, including Bill Cartwright, Horace Grant, Luc Longley, Toni Kukoc, Dennis Rodman, B.J. Armstrong, John Paxson, Steve Kerr, and Ron Harper.

LEFT: Michael Jordan was nicknamed "Air" for his amazing ability to hang above the rim. **ABOVE**: Scottie Pippen had the talent to match Jordan.

Chicago made another great move by hiring Phil Jackson to coach the team. He taught the Bulls to share the ball on offense, which created opportunities for everyone to score. Chicago's unselfish style of play helped the team win the NBA championship six times. The Bulls might have won even more had Jordan not left the game for most of two seasons to try his hand at professional baseball. He returned to Chicago to win three more NBA scoring titles.

After Jordan retired, Chicago fans knew they would never see a player of his *caliber* again. However, the chemistry that made the championship teams of the 1990s so special was something the Bulls were able to copy. In the years after Jordan left, Chicago brought in Luol Deng, Kirk Hinrich, Ben Gordon, Joakim Noah, Carlos Boozer, Taj Gibson, Jimmy Butler, and Derrick Rose. Each player offered something unique to the Bulls. They all worked hard to be good teammates.

Among these players, Rose was a true standout. Like Jordan, he could take over a game and lift his team to victory. Rose also had a talent for bringing out the best in his teammates. In 2010–11, the Bulls won 62 games and found themselves in a familiar place—fighting for a spot in the NBA Finals. Although they narrowly missed a return

trip to the championship series, Bulls fans knew that another title was within their grasp.

LEFT: Phil Jackson shows off his Coach of the Year trophy after the 1995–96 season.   **ABOVE**: Derrick Rose looks for an opening in the defense.

Home Court

The Bulls play in an arena located on the west side of Chicago. It was built in 1994 and is also home to the Blackhawks hockey club. Before moving to their new arena on Madison Street, both teams played their home games in Chicago Stadium, which was also located on Madison Street. The old building was so loud during games that it was nicknamed the "Madhouse on Madison."

The Bulls' new arena was built to remind fans of Chicago Stadium. The outside of the building has the same feel as the old one. The inside was designed to *amplify* the crowd noise. It is still one of the loudest arenas in the United States.

BY THE NUMBERS

- The Bulls' arena has 20,917 seats for basketball.
- The arena cost $175 million to build.
- As of 2013–14, the Bulls had retired four jersey numbers—4 (Jerry Sloan), 10 (Bob Love), 23 (Michael Jordan), and 33 (Scottie Pippen). The team has also honored coach Phil Jackson and General Manager Jerry Krause, who helped build the Bulls into a championship club.

The Bulls' arena is one of the best in the NBA for watching a game.

Dressed for Success

The Bulls have always worn red, white, and black. In the late 1960s, they featured warm-ups that also included the color pink. During the 1990s, the Bulls wore **pinstriped** uniforms. They also started wearing black shoes during the playoffs. This has since become a team tradition.

The Bulls were named in honor of the Chicago Stockyards, where much of America's beef once came from. The team's founder, Dick Klein, wanted a **logo** that showed "a bull in a fight." The result was a red and black bull with red eyes and blood on the tips of his horns. Chicago's logo has changed little since then.

BOB
LOVE
forward
CHICAGO

LEFT: Carlos Boozer heads up the court in Chicago's 2013–14 home uniform.
ABOVE: As this trading card of Bob Love shows, the Bulls used pink as a team color in the 1960s.

No player would ever turn down a chance to take the court beside Michael Jordan. However, for many years, the biggest obstacle to Chicago's championship hopes was finding the right group of players to surround Jordan. When Phil Jackson became the Bulls' coach in 1989, he gave his players clearer roles. He also taught Jordan how to help his teammates shine.

The Bulls were already very good. Their roster included big men Horace Grant and Bill Cartwright and guards B.J. Armstrong and John Paxson. The team's most dynamic player after Jordan was Scottie Pippen. In the spring of 1991, the Bulls finally won their first championship. After beating the Detroit Pistons in the **Eastern Conference Finals**, they defeated the Los Angeles Lakers in five games to take the title.

One year later, the Bulls returned to the NBA Finals and played the Portland Trail Blazers for the title. Fans were excited to see a showdown between Jordan and Clyde Drexler. It turned out to be a mismatch. The Portland star simply could not stop Jordan. After

Once Phil Jackson taught Michael Jordan how to be a leader, the Bulls became nearly unstoppable.

Chicago's six-game victory, Drexler said, "Going into the series, I thought Michael had two thousand moves. I was wrong—he has three thousand!"

The 1993 NBA Finals brought Jordan and the Bulls face-to-face with Charles Barkley and the Phoenix Suns. The two stars fought hard, and after five games the Bulls were ahead in the series. The Suns would not give up. They led Game 6 by two points with just a few seconds to go. Chicago fans were worried their third championship might be slipping away, but the Bulls weren't. Jordan got the ball and passed to Pippen. When he couldn't find an open

shot, he passed to Grant, who saw Paxson standing alone beyond the 3-point line and whipped the ball to him. Paxson took a long shot that swished through the net to give the Bulls their championship "three-peat."

The Bulls returned to the NBA Finals three years later after steamrolling through the regular season with a record of 72–10. Jordan and Pippen were still the club's stars. Their new teammates included Dennis Rodman, Toni Kukoc, Ron Harper, Luc Longley, and Steve Kerr. They easily defeated the Seattle Supersonics for their fourth championship.

In the 1997 NBA Finals, the Bulls battled the Utah Jazz. Again, just one win from the title, Chicago faced a tense situation in Game 6. With time ticking away late in the fourth quarter, the score was tied, 86–86. Everyone in the building knew Jordan would get the ball. He faked out three Utah players and then suddenly fired a pass to Kerr, who had been ice-cold during the series. Kerr calmly swished a 20-foot shot for the victory.

History repeated itself one year and one day later, as Jordan again helped beat the Jazz in Game 6 of the NBA Finals. This time, he made the winning shot himself. With the Bulls behind 86–85 and less than 10 seconds on the clock, Jordan faked to the basket, then quickly stopped and rose for a jump shot. As the ball went through the basket, Jordan punched the air in a joyous victory celebration. It was the last shot he would ever take for the Bulls, who had their sixth NBA championship in eight remarkable seasons.

LEFT: There was no debate about the NBA's best team after the 1995–96 season. **ABOVE**: Steve Kerr watches his shot swish through the net in the final seconds of Game 6 in the 1997 NBA Finals.

Go-To Guys

To be a true star in the NBA, you need more than a great shot. You have to be a "go-to guy"—someone teammates trust to make the winning play when the seconds are ticking away in a big game. Bulls fans have had a lot to cheer about over the years, including these great stars …

THE PIONEERS

JERRY SLOAN   6′ 5″ Guard

• BORN: 3/28/1942   • PLAYED FOR TEAM: 1966–67 TO 1975–76

Jerry Sloan played every game as if it was his last. That helped him become one of the best defenders in the NBA. In 10 seasons with the Bulls, Sloan averaged nearly 15 points a game and made the league's **All-Defensive Team** six times.

BOB LOVE   6′ 8″ Forward

• BORN: 12/8/1942   • PLAYED FOR TEAM: 1968–69 TO 1976–77

Players who matched up against Bob Love never got a rest. He could score from anywhere on the court and was a great defensive player. Love averaged more than 25 points a game twice and was named an **All-Star** three times.

CHET WALKER
6′ 7″ Forward

- BORN: 2/22/1940   • PLAYED FOR TEAM: 1969–70 TO 1974–75

Chet Walker was nicknamed the "Jet" because of his speed and leaping ability. He often provided important points at "crunch time." Walker was one of the best free-throw shooters in team history.

NORM VAN LIER
6′ 2″ Guard

- BORN: 4/1/1947   • DIED: 2/26/2009
- PLAYED FOR TEAM: 1971–72 TO 1977–78

Norm Van Lier was a *tenacious* defensive player and an unselfish passer. The Bulls drafted him in 1969, traded him, and then spent several years trying to get him back. When Van Lier retired, he ranked first in team history in assists.

ARTIS GILMORE
7′ 2″ Center

- BORN: 9/21/1948   • PLAYED FOR TEAM: 1976–77 TO 1981–82 & 1987–88

Artis Gilmore came to the Bulls after the **American Basketball Association** folded in 1976. Few players in the NBA could match his strength. He was an All-Star four times with the Bulls.

REGGIE THEUS
6′ 7″ Guard

- BORN: 10/13/1957   • PLAYED FOR TEAM: 1978–79 TO 1983–84

Few Bulls played with more energy than Reggie Theus. He was one of the tallest guards of his era, as well as one of the finest shooters and passers. Theus represented the Bulls in the **All-Star Game** twice.

ABOVE: Norm Van Lier

MICHAEL JORDAN   6′ 6″ Guard

- BORN: 2/17/1963
- PLAYED FOR TEAM: 1984–85 TO 1992–93 & 1994–95 TO 1997–98

Many fans consider Michael Jordan the greatest player in NBA history. He led Chicago to six championships and was named **Most Valuable Player (MVP)** of the NBA Finals each time. No player has ever captured the world's imagination as Jordan did. No one could match his desire to win.

SCOTTIE PIPPEN   6′ 8″ Guard/Forward

- BORN: 9/25/1965   • PLAYED FOR TEAM: 1987–88 TO 1997–98 & 2003–04

Scottie Pippen had the talent to play every position on the court, and

sometimes he did. His ability to guard an opponent's best player was a key to the Bulls' six championships. Pippen was voted to the NBA's All-Defensive Team 10 times.

HORACE GRANT   6′ 10″ Forward

- BORN: 7/4/1965
- PLAYED FOR TEAM: 1987–88 TO 1993–94

Horace Grant was one of the best defensive players and rebounders in the NBA. If teams paid too much attention to Jordan and Pippen, Grant chipped in with baskets from the outside. His identical twin, Harvey, was also an NBA player.

LUOL DENG   6′ 9″ Forward

- BORN: 4/16/1985   • PLAYED FOR TEAM: 2004–05 TO 2013–14

Luol Deng played just one season in college before coming to the
Bulls. He needed only a few games before he looked like an old pro.
A member of Sudan's Dinka tribe, Deng
learned basketball from Manute Bol, another
Dinka tribesman who starred in the NBA for
many years.

JOAKIM NOAH   6′ 11″ Center

- BORN: 2/25/1985

- FIRST SEASON WITH TEAM: 2007–08

The Bulls like players with championship
experience. Joakim Noah led his college team to
two national championships before coming to
Chicago. Noah helped the Bulls win **division**
titles in 2011 and 2013. He made the All-
Defensive Team in both seasons.

DERRICK ROSE   6′ 3″ Guard

- BORN: 10/4/1988   • FIRST SEASON WITH TEAM: 2008–09

Derrick Rose grew up in Chicago as a huge fan of the Bulls. When the
team drafted him in the first round in 2008, it was a dream come true.
Rose became the third Bull to win Rookie of the Year. In 2010–11, he
led the Bulls to their first 60-win season since the 1990s and was named
league MVP.

LEFT: Horace Grant   **ABOVE**: Joakim Noah

Calling the Shots

The Bulls have never been a dull team. Perhaps that is because they have always hired coaches with exciting new ideas. Johnny Kerr was Chicago's first coach. He believed that the key to success was creating difficult match-ups for opponents. He was named **Coach of the Year** in his first season.

Dick Motta followed Kerr. He had a simple rule for his players: as long as they played hard defense, he would keep them on the court. The Bulls quickly became the best defensive team in the league. Chicago made the playoffs six years in a row starting in 1969–70, and reached the conference finals twice.

During the 1980s, Doug Collins began building a championship **contender** in Chicago. In 1989, the team hired Phil Jackson to finish the job. The Bulls had loads of talent, but they lost to the Detroit Pistons in the playoffs year after year. Jackson spent as much time working on the confidence and attitude of his players as he did on their shooting and passing.

Of course, Jackson had some exciting ideas on how the Bulls should play, too. For years, the team had expected Michael Jordan

Dick Motta is surrounded by his starting five in 1972—Chet Walker, Jerry Sloan, Tom Boerwinkle, Bob Weiss, and Bob Love.

to be the hero every night. Chicago's opponents expected this, too. Jackson and assistant coach Tex Winter designed plays that would use the talents of every player on the floor. They called their system the "Triangle Offense." It helped the Bulls win six championships.

After Jordan left the Bulls, the challenge for Chicago coaches was to come up with a totally new system for the team. This was easier said than done. In 2010–11, Tom Thibodeau began calling the shots, and the Bulls won two division titles in a row. Thibodeau was known as a defensive genius. As an assistant for the New York Knicks and Boston Celtics, he helped both teams reach the NBA Finals. In his first season with the Bulls, Thibodeau joined Kerr, Motta, and Jackson as Chicago leaders to win NBA Coach of the Year.

One Great Day

When Michael Jordan joined the Bulls in 1984, he was on a roll. He had just led the U.S. basketball team to a gold medal in the *Olympics*. Two years earlier, he had guided the University of North Carolina to the college national championship. Naturally, he assumed that winning an NBA title would be the next step.

In the spring of 1991, the Bulls finally reached the NBA Finals. Coach Phil Jackson had drilled home an important lesson to Jordan: the key to winning was getting the entire team to play together. Jordan and his teammates were eager to take on the Los Angeles Lakers. When the series started, the Lakers were only worried about Jordan. They quickly learned that the Bulls were a complete team. Chicago won three of the first four games.

By Game 5, Los Angeles had no idea how to beat the Bulls. Chicago won the clincher easily, 108–101, to claim the first

Michael Jordan is surrounded by four of his championship teammates—
John Paxson, Bill Cartwright, Scottie Pippen, and Horace Grant—
after Chicago's first championship.

championship in team history. Almost everyone on the Bulls contributed to the victory. Scottie Pippen led the team with 32 points and 13 rebounds. Bill Cartwright had seven assists, and Horace Grant scored 11 points. John Paxson made five baskets in the last four minutes and finished with 20 points.

And Jordan? All he did was score 30 points with 10 assists and five steals. An hour after the game ended, he still had tears in his eyes. "I never thought I'd be this emotional," Jordan said. "I always had faith I'd get this ring one day."

Legend Has It

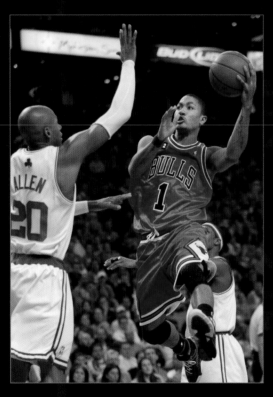

Did Michael Jordan have the best playoff debut in team history?

LEGEND HAS IT that he did *not*. That honor belongs to Derrick Rose. In 2008–09, Rose faced the Boston Celtics in the first playoff game of his career. Going head-to-head with defensive star Rajon Rondo, Rose scored 36 points and had 11 assists. The Bulls beat the Celtics on their home court in **overtime**, 105–103. Rose's 36 points tied the record for a rookie in his first playoff game, which had been set in 1970 by Kareem Abdul-Jabbar.

ABOVE: Derrick Rose's first playoff appearance was a memorable one. This photo shows him floating to the basket for a layup during that game.

ho made the Bulls' greatest "orgotten" shot?

LEGEND HAS IT that Bill Wennington did. After Michael ordan came out of retirement in 1995, his first big test came against the New York Knicks at Madison Square Garden. Jordan had looked a little rusty in his first few games, but against the Knicks he scored 55 points. With the score tied 111–111, everyone expected Jordan to take the last shot. When the Knicks double-teamed him, Jordan shoveled the ball to Wennington, who made the winning dunk. "How about that?" Wennington told reporters afterward. "Michael and I combined for 57 points!"

ere the 1966–67 Bulls the best st-year team in NBA history?

LEGEND HAS IT that they were. The Bulls won their first three games, defeating the St. Louis Hawks, San Francisco Warriors, and Los Angeles Lakers. Chicago finished the year with 33 victories and made the playoffs. Guards Guy Rodgers and Jerry Sloan played in the All-Star Game, and Rodgers led the NBA in assists. Center Erwin Mueller was named to the **All-Rookie Team**. And Johnny Kerr was named Coach of the Year.

It Really Happened

During their six championship seasons, the Bulls were known for their great balance. The team didn't appear to have a weakness. Chicago could outrun and outscore opponents or win tough defensive struggles.

It took a while to put this team together. Fortunately, Chicago had two amazing building blocks: Michael Jordan and Scottie Pippen. The duo provided match-up problems for every team the Bulls faced. Their first year playing together as starters was 1988–89, and it didn't take long to show the rest of the NBA that they were something very special.

In a January game that season against the Los Angeles Clippers, Chicago fans were treated to a thrilling battle. The teams were tied after one quarter, and the Clippers held a one-point lead at halftime. Los Angeles built a four-point lead in the fourth quarter, but the Bulls sent the game into overtime. They went on to win, 126–121.

After the game, fans noticed something extremely unusual. Jordan scored 41 points and added 11 assists and 10 rebounds. But Pippen also reached double-figures in three categories, with

Scottie Pippen and Michael Jordan celebrate one of their six NBA championships. They are the only pair of Chicago teammates to record triple-doubles in the same game.

15 points, 12 assists, and 10 rebounds. It marked the first time in history that two Bulls had "triple-doubles" in the same game.

In the years that followed, the Bulls added more players who—like Jordan and Pippen—could do many things well. Amazingly, however, no Chicago duo has recorded triple-doubles in the same game again.

Team Spirit

Chicago basketball fans are some of the toughest in sports. They cheer hard for the Bulls, and support them through good times and bad times. The team rewards their loyalty in many ways. Benny the Bull, a big red mascot, roams the stands and sidelines. He also performs dunking exhibitions and other stunts. The Luvabulls dance team takes the floor during breaks in the action to entertain the crowd.

For many years, the loudest cheers at Bulls games were often saved for the Matadors, one of the strangest cheerleading squads in all of sports. The Matadors were made up of Chicago's "biggest" basketball fans. This group of large men would thunder onto the court during timeouts and dance for about a minute. The Matadors brought smiles—and looks of wonder—to thousands of faces at every Bulls game.

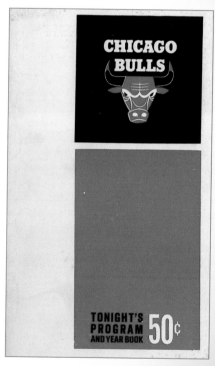

LEFT: Benny the Bull
ABOVE: This program was on sale during Chicago's first season.

Timeline

The basketball season is played from October through June. That means each season takes place at the end of one year and the beginning of the next. In this timeline, the accomplishments of the Bulls are shown by season.

1970–71
Chet Walker is the NBA's best free-throw shooter.

1986–87
Michael Jordan scores 40 or more points nine games in a row.

1966–67
The Bulls play their first season.

1981–82
Artis Gilmore leads the NBA in **field goal percentage**.

1990–91
The Bulls win their first NBA championship.

Jerry Sloan takes a free throw. He was one of the team's first stars.

Ben
Gordon

1992–93
The Bulls
complete their
first championship
"three-peat."

2004–05
Ben Gordon is named
Sixth Man of the Year.

2010–11
Tom Thibodeau is
named Coach of the Year.

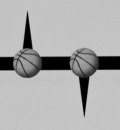

1993–94
Scottie Pippen is
named All-Star
Game MVP.

1997–98
The Bulls win their sixth
NBA championship.

2013–14
Joakim Noah is
named Defensive
Player of the Year.

Scottie
Pippen

Joakim
Noah

Fun Facts

COMING UP ROSES

When 20-year-old Derrick Rose won the Skills Challenge at the 2009 All-Star Game, he was the first rookie ever to win that event. Two years later, at 22, he became the youngest player to be named league MVP.

LONG SHOT

In a game against the San Antonio Spurs, Norm Van Lier set a team record by making a basket from 84 feet away. His shot came at the end of the first quarter. "When it got past half-court," he said later, "I just knew it was going in."

FATHER TIME

If Joakim Noah enters the **Hall of Fame** one day, he won't be the first member of his family to do so. His father, Yannick Noah, was the number-one tennis player in the world in 1986 and entered the International Tennis Hall of Fame in 2005.

Michael Jordan's return from retirement was front-page news. So was his choice of uniform number 45.

NUMBERS GAME

Chicago's most famous uniform may be the one that Michael Jordan wore after he came back from a brief retirement. The Bulls had retired his number 23, so he chose number 45 instead. When he changed back to 23 during the 1995 playoffs, the NBA fined the Bulls for switching the number without the league's approval. Jordan wore 23 for the rest of his career.

AN APPETITE FOR WINNING

The Bulls' success in the 1990s was great for Chicago food lovers. Hungry sellout crowds pouring out of the arena helped turn Randolph Street into one of the city's most popular restaurant districts.

CHAIRMEN OF THE BOARDS

Two Bulls have led the league in rebounding—Dennis Rodman and Charles Oakley. Rodman did it three seasons in a row starting in 1995–96. Chicago won the NBA championship each year.

Talking Basketball

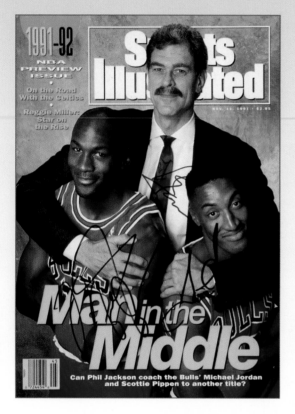

1991-92 NBA PREVIEW ISSUE

On the Road With the Celtics

Reggie Miller: Star on the Rise

Sports Illustrated

Man in the Middle

Can Phil Jackson coach the Bulls' Michael Jordan and Scottie Pippen to another title?

"We weren't battling the Pistons—we were battling ourselves in some respect. "

▶ **Phil Jackson,** *on the mental challenge of reaching the NBA Finals*

"Talent wins games, but teamwork and intelligence win championships."

▶ **Michael Jordan,** *on what made the Bulls so tough in the playoffs*

"What I pride myself on as a player is my preparation, making sure that I do the right things to be in a position to do what's necessary for the team."

▶ **Ben Gordon,** *on the key to being a good sixth man*

"We scared a lot of people in that five-year run. That was the team that kind of laid the foundation for basketball in Chicago."

▶ **Chet Walker,** *on the Bulls of the early 1970s*

"He was an inspiration to me as a basketball player and as a person."

▶ **Scottie Pippen,** *on former coach and broadcaster Johnny Kerr*

"It was great hearing my name and being the number one pick."

▶ **Derrick Rose,** *on realizing his dream of playing for the Bulls*

"Saving a basket is just as good as making one."

▶ **Jerry Sloan,** *on the importance of playing tough defense*

LEFT: The signatures of Michael Jordan, Phil Jackson, and Scottie Pippen make this magazine a great collector's item.   **ABOVE**: Chet Walker

Great Debates

People who root for the Bulls love to compare their favorite moments, teams, and players. Some debates have been going on for years! How would you settle these classic basketball arguments?

Toni Kukoc was the Bulls' best sixth man . . .

. . . because he could play five positions. Kukoc (**LEFT**) lined up at small forward most games, but at 6'11" he could also fill in at power forward and center. Kukoc's accurate outside shot allowed him to play shooting guard, and from time to time, he even brought the ball up the court as the point guard. Kukoc was Chicago's sixth man in three of his first four NBA seasons. In 1995–96, he was named NBA Sixth Man of the Year.

Are you forgetting Ben Gordon? He was the team's best sixth man . . .

. . . because he was voted the NBA's best sixth man as a 21-year-old rookie. Gordon started only three games in 2004–05, but he was Chicago's leading scorer, with 1,235 points. Though Gordon later became a starter for the Bulls, he continued to be a powerhouse coming off the bench. In 2006–07, Gordon scored 40 points as a substitute twice in one week!

.. because he scored 63 points against one of the greatest teams in NBA history. No one expected the Bulls to win a game against Boston. The Celtics had five players ticketed for the Hall of Fame. But nothing could stop Jordan. He torched the Celtics—on their own home court! What was the most amazing thing about this night? Jordan was still recovering from a foot injury that had kept him out of 64 games!

Hold on. Jordan's "Flu Game" was far more amazing . . .

.. because it came during the 1997 NBA Finals. Heading into Game 5, the Bulls and Utah Jazz were tied in the series. Jordan was suffering from dizziness and a weak stomach all game long. He had food poisoning from a pizza the night before. At one point during the game, Scottie Pippen had to hold Jordan up (RIGHT). Somehow, Jordan pulled it together and scored 38 points to give the Bulls a 90–88 victory. They went on to win Game 6 for their fifth NBA title. Jordan later said the Flu Game was the toughest of his life.

The great Bulls teams and players have left their marks on the record books. These are the "best of the best" …

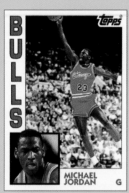

Michael Jordan

Elton Brand

BULLS AWARD WINNERS

ROOKIE OF THE YEAR

Michael Jordan	1984–85
Elton Brand	1999–00*
Derrick Rose	2008–09

NBA FINALS MVP

Michael Jordan	1990–91
Michael Jordan	1991–92
Michael Jordan	1992–93
Michael Jordan	1995–96
Michael Jordan	1996–97
Michael Jordan	1997–98

SLAM DUNK CHAMPION

Michael Jordan	1986–87
Michael Jordan	1987–88

NBA MVP

Michael Jordan	1987–88
Michael Jordan	1990–91
Michael Jordan	1991–92
Michael Jordan	1995–96
Michael Jordan	1997–98
Derrick Rose	2010–11

ALL-STAR GAME MVP

Michael Jordan	1987–88
Scottie Pippen	1993–94
Michael Jordan	1995–96

SIXTH MAN AWARD

Toni Kukoc	1995–96
Ben Gordon	2004–05

COACH OF THE YEAR

Johnny Kerr	1966–67
Dick Motta	1970–71
Phil Jackson	1995–96
Tom Thibodeau	2010–11

DEFENSIVE PLAYER OF THE YEAR

Michael Jordan	1987–88
Joakim Noah	2013–14

3-POINT SHOOTOUT CHAMPION

Craig Hodges	1989–90
Craig Hodges	1990–91
Craig Hodges	1991–92
Steve Kerr	1996–97

Shared the award with another player.

BULLS ACHIEVEMENTS

ACHIEVEMENT	SEASON
Midwest Division Champions	1974–75
Central Division Champions	1990–91
Eastern Conference Champions	1990–91
NBA Champions	1990–91
Central Division Champions	1991–92
Eastern Conference Champions	1991–92
NBA Champions	1991–92
Central Division Champions	1992–93
Eastern Conference Champions	1992–93
NBA Champions	1992–93
Central Division Champions	1995–96
Eastern Conference Champions	1995–96
NBA Champions	1995–96
Central Division Champions	1996–97
Eastern Conference Champions	1996–97
NBA Champions	1996–97
Central Division Champions	1997–98
Eastern Conference Champions	1997–98
NBA Champions	1997–98
Central Division Champions	2010–11
Central Division Champions	2011–12

Jerry Sloan was a star for the 1974–75 Bulls.

Dennis Rodman helped the team win three titles in the mid-1990s.

This pennant celebrated Chicago's first "three-peat."

Pinpoints

The history of a basketball team is made up of many smaller stories. These stories take place all over the map—not just in the city a team calls "home." Match the pushpins on these maps to the **TEAM FACTS**, and you will begin to see the story of the Bulls unfold!

TEAM FACTS

1   Chicago, Illinois—*The Bulls have played here since 1966.*
2   Sioux City, Iowa—*Kirk Hinrich was born here.*
3   Benton Harbor, Michigan—*Chet Walker was born here.*
4   East Liverpool, Ohio—*Norm Van Lier was born here.*
5   Brooklyn, New York—*Michael Jordan was born here.*
6   Hamburg, Arkansas—*Scottie Pippen was born here.*
7   Bastrop, Louisiana—*Bob Love was born here.*
8   Los Angeles, California—*The Bulls won their first NBA championship here.*
9   Houston, Texas—*Jimmy Butler was born here.*
10   Aschaffenburg, Germany—*Carlos Boozer was born here.*
11   Split, Croatia—*Toni Kukoc was born here.*
12   Wau, Sudan—*Luol Deng was born here.*

Bob Love

45

Glossary

🏀 **ALL-DEFENSIVE TEAM**—The annual honor given to the NBA's best defensive players at each position.

🏀 **ALL-ROOKIE TEAM**—The annual honor given to the NBA's best first-year players at each position.

🏀 **ALL-STAR**—A player selected to play in the annual All-Star Game.

🏀 **ALL-STAR GAME**—The annual game in which the best players from the East and the West play against each other.

🏀 **AMERICAN BASKETBALL ASSOCIATION**—The basketball league that played for nine seasons starting in 1967.

🧠 *AMPLIFY*—Increase.

🏀 **ASSISTS**—Passes that lead to baskets.

🧠 *CALIBER*—A level of excellence.

🧠 *CENTURY*—A period of 100 years.

🏀 **COACH OF THE YEAR**—The annual award given to the league's best coach.

🏀 **CONTENDER**—A team that competes for a championship.

🏀 **DIVISION**—A group of teams within a league that play in the same part of the country.

🏀 **DRAFT**—The annual meeting during which NBA teams choose from a group of the best college and foreign players.

🏀 **EASTERN CONFERENCE**—A group of teams that play in the East. The winner of the Eastern Conference meets the winner of the Western Conference in the league finals.

🏀 **EASTERN CONFERENCE FINALS**—The playoff series that determines which team from the Eastern Conference will play the best team from the Western Conference for the NBA championship.

🧠 *ERA*—A period of time in history.

🏀 **EXPANSION CLUB**—A new team that joins a league already in business.

🏀 **FIELD GOAL PERCENTAGE**—A statistic that measures shooting accuracy.

🏀 **HALL OF FAME**—The museum in Springfield, Massachusetts where basketball's greatest players are honored.

🧠 *LOGO*—A symbol or design that represents a company or team.

🏀 **MOST VALUABLE PLAYER (MVP)**—The annual award given to the league's best player; also given to the best player in the league finals and All-Star Game.

🏀 **NATIONAL BASKETBALL ASSOCIATION (NBA)**—The professional league that has been operating since 1946–47.

🏀 **NBA FINALS**—The playoff series that decides the champion of the league.

🧠 *OLYMPICS*—An international sports competition held every four years.

🏀 **OVERTIME**—The extra period played when a game is tied after 48 minutes.

🧠 *PINSTRIPED*—A design with thin stripes.

🏀 **PLAYOFFS**—The games played after the season to determine the league champion.

🏀 **PROFESSIONAL**—A player or team that plays a sport for money.

🏀 **ROOKIE OF THE YEAR**—The annual award given to the league's best first-year player.

🏀 **SIXTH MAN OF THE YEAR**—The annual award given to the league's best player off the bench.

🧠 *TENACIOUS*—Refusing to give up.

🧠 *TRADITION*—A belief or custom that is handed down from generation to generation.

FAST BREAK

TEAM SPIRIT introduces a great way to stay up to date with your team! Visit our **FAST BREAK** link and get connected to the latest and greatest updates. **FAST BREAK** serves as a young reader's ticket to an exclusive web page—with more stories, fun facts, team records, and photos of the Bulls. Content is updated during and after each season. The **FAST BREAK** feature also enables readers to send comments and letters to the author! Log onto:

www.norwoodhousepress.com/library.aspx

and click on the tab: **TEAM SPIRIT** to access **FAST BREAK**.

Read all the books in the series to learn more about professional sports. For a complete listing of the baseball, basketball, football, and hockey teams in the **TEAM SPIRIT** series, visit our website at:

www.norwoodhousepress.com/library.aspx

On the Road

CHICAGO BULLS
1901 West Madison Street
Chicago, Illinois 60612
(312) 455-4000
www.bulls.com

NAISMITH MEMORIAL
BASKETBALL HALL OF FAME
1000 West Columbus Avenue
Springfield, Massachusetts 01105
(877) 4HOOPLA
www.hoophall.com

On the Bookshelf

To learn more about the sport of basketball, look for these books at your library or bookstore:

• Doeden, Matt. *Basketball Legends In the Making*. North Mankato, Minnesota: Capstone Press, 2014.

• Rappaport, Ken. *Basketball's Top 10 Slam Dunkers*. Berkeley Heights, New Jersey: Enslow Publishers, 2013.

• Silverman, Drew. *The NBA Finals*. Minneapolis, Minnesota: ABDO Group, 2013.

Index

PAGE NUMBERS IN **BOLD** REFER TO ILLUSTRATIONS.

THE TEAM

MARK STEWART has written more than 40 books on basketball, and over 150 sports books for kids. He grew up in New York City during the 1960s rooting for the Knicks and Nets, and was lucky enough to meet many of the stars of those teams. Mark comes from a family of writers. His grandfather was Sunday Editor of *The New York Times* and his mother was Articles Editor of *The Ladies' Home Journal* and *McCall's*. Mark has profiled hundreds of athletes over the last 20 years. He has also written several books about his native New York, and New Jersey, his home today. Mark is a graduate of Duke University, with a degree in History. He lives with his daughters and wife Sarah overlooking Sandy Hook, New Jersey.